Original title:
In the Heart of Paradise

Copyright © 2025 Creative Arts Management OÜ
All rights reserved.

Author: Sophia Kingsley
ISBN HARDBACK: 978-1-80581-475-7
ISBN PAPERBACK: 978-1-80581-002-5
ISBN EBOOK: 978-1-80581-475-7

Unveiling the Enchantment

A squirrel in a top hat, quite the sight,
Holding tea with a rabbit, oh what a delight!
The daisies are gossiping, sharing their news,
While the tulips are giggling, in colorful hues.

A butterfly sneezes, causing chaos to reign,
As ants form a parade, wearing clowns' disdain.
The sun beams a grin, as bright as can be,
While shadows dance about, like they're wild and free.

Mushrooms are dancing to a tune from the past,
The daisies, they sway, hoping this fun will last.
A hedgehog in sunglasses, a star of the show,
Winks at the beetles, as they put on a glow.

Mistakes with the bees, they flew with such flair,
One landed on a gnome, who just gave a stare.
Yet laughter erupts, in this joyful affair,
While frolicsome friends fill the warm, sunny air.

Mystic Trails through Dappled Light

A raccoon on roller skates zooms down the lane,
Chasing after fairies, who burst out in sprain.
The mushrooms are chuckling, their caps in a twist,
While leaves shout for help, like they know they've been missed.

A wobbly tree sings, it's a real funny song,
Its branches are flailing, as if they belong.
The sunlight is giggling, it tickles each petal,
As dragonflies swoosh, in a whimsical medal.

Frogs croak in chorus, with voices so grand,
Joining in harmony, in this silly band.
An owl in a bow tie, looks dapper and proud,
While snickers from critters echo, oh so loud!

They dance and they prance under skies so blue,
Where laughter is golden, and friendship is true.
With all of this mischief, the day disappears,
But joy lingers still, through the laughter and cheers.

Garden of Forgotten Echoes

In the garden of giggles, the sun's taking bets,
On cucumbers dancing and speedy omelets.
The flowers are snickering, quite clever and spry,
As the wind blows a riddle, that makes daisies fly.

Old gnomes play poker, with cards made of leaves,
While bees wear sombreros, in search of sweet heaves.
A snail pulls a wagon, so stylish, you'll see,
With a sign on the back that says, "Catch up with me!"

The carrots are laughing, they're digging a hole,
Trying to hide from let's say, the playful mole.
While radishes tell tales of starry-eyed dreams,
Underneath the wide sky, with laughter that beams.

As echoes of merriment drift through the air,
The garden's alive with sprightly affair.
In this whimsical space where nothing is strict,
The sounds of pure joy and silliness conflict.

Underneath the Arc of Rainbows

A squirrel twirled on a sunflower,
Chasing shadows with wild power.
He slipped and fell in the muddy lane,
Now he's a rainbow with a touch of stain.

The birds laugh hard from the branch above,
With beaks a-chatter, they call it love.
As the wind tickles the leaves so free,
They sing of a squirrel's muddled spree.

Mosaic of Dreams

A dreamer tossed her socks in the air,
Hoping to catch a slice of fair.
Two left feet danced under the moon,
While the cat judged with a skeptical tune.

Colors mixed as paint spilled wide,
The world turned into a wobbly ride.
Even the goldfish wore a crown,
Waving hello as they swam upside down.

Soliloquy of Butterflies

Butterflies wear hats in shades so bright,
Debating who serenades best at night.
They sip on nectar with centuries old grace,
Swapping stories of their favorite place.

One brought glitter and another brought jam,
A party in petals, oh what a sham!
They twirled and swirled on a breeze so bold,
With laughter that sparkled like shards of gold.

Bountiful Secrets of the Glade

In a glade filled with mushrooms and cheer,
A rabbit told secrets that none could hear.
With a nibble of grass and a wink of an eye,
He claimed he'd outsmarted the moon in the sky.

The frogs in the pond joined in the fun,
Croaking tales of the races they've run.
With every splash, they cheered and they crooned,
As the stars above began to balloon.

Harmonies in Twilight

As the sun dips low, a giggle takes flight,
Bouncing off clouds, in the fading light.
Silly shadows dance with a sprightly cheer,
Even the stars wave, "It's almost time, dear!"

Crickets join in with their quirky refrain,
A symphony played with delight and disdain.
Fireflies blink like they're stuck in a trance,
Good luck keeping step with their wobbly dance!

Whispered Treasures

Hidden jewels gleam in the grass below,
A wallet of snacks, don't ask where they go!
Squirrels trade secrets, wearing tiny crowns,
While gossiping flowers share the latest downs.

Laughter bubbles up through the emerald sea,
A fountain of giggles, what a sight to see!
Even the leaves high above in the trees,
Might spill the tea on the flapping nape breeze!

Song of the Wandering Breeze

The wind plays tricks, like a mischievous elf,
Whispers of mischief, don't ask for help.
Balloons float away, in a whimsical chase,
While kites join the fray, with a comical grace.

Riding on currents, the giggles take flight,
Laughter wraps round like a blanket of light.
From petals to puddles, the mirth takes a spin,
Nature conspires, let the games begin!

Labyrinths of Light

Lost in a maze of a sunbeam's embrace,
Rabbits wear sunglasses, in this funny place.
Twisting and turning, they hop with such flair,
Chasing their shadows well beyond any dare.

Each turn brings a wink from a mischievous hare,
Who plays hide and seek with delight in the air.
The sun grins and winks, like a jester put forth,
In a world turned around, we find endless worth!

The Allure of Untamed Beauty

Upon the hill, a goat in a hat,
He thinks he's the king, imagine that!
Flowers giggle, swaying with grace,
While bees take selfies, buzzing in space.

A squirrel on a branch, reads the news,
Accidentally spills his berry stews.
Laughter echoes through the vast green lane,
Nature's circus, wild and insane.

Cradled by the Skies

Clouds like pillows, fluffy and bright,
Birds throw parties, in morning light.
A kite takes a dive, gives us a scare,
While a dog in shades lounges, without a care!

Sunsets wink, color the town,
As bats don capes, and swoosh around.
Nature's jesters in vibrant display,
Underneath the celestial ballet.

The Kaleidoscope of Seasons

Spring sneezes flowers, they giggle and bloom,
While winter throws snowballs and fills every room.
Summer flips burgers, a sizzle, a pop,
Autumn juggles pumpkins, right on the top!

Every season, a prankster at play,
Making us laugh in the silliest way.
Through each twist, a colorful scene,
Life's a parade, so merry, so keen.

Blossoming Horizons

A tulip in shorts, struts down the lane,
Waving to daisies, in a joyous refrain.
The skyplays peek-a-boo, with sun beams so sly,
While grass tickles toes, as we pass by!

Butterflies tango, on a breezy whim,
Frogs croak choruses, voices so grim.
Yet laughter prevails in this whimsical land,
Nature's giggles, all perfectly planned.

Where the Wildflowers Sing

Beneath the sky of purple hues,
The flowers gossip, sharing news.
Bees wear tuxedos, oh what a show,
While butterflies dance in a comical flow.

A dandelion puff, a wish turned to jest,
Said, "Life's too short, so laugh with the rest!"
The bumblebees buzz in a chorus divine,
As ants hold a feast—politely, they dine.

Lullabies of the Flowing Brook

The brook sings softly, a splashing tune,
While fish take turns in a synchronized swoon.
They slip and they slide in their watery race,
While frogs take bets, 'Oh, what a pace!'

A willow tree chuckles, swaying so low,
Telling secrets to stones, all in the flow.
'Catch me those ripples,' he teases the breeze,
'Life's like a river, just flow and appease!'

A Serenade of Sunlight

Sunbeams pirouette, they twirl in delight,
As squirrels wear sunglasses, a comical sight.
The daisies all giggle, their heads held so high,
While shadows play tricks as they wave goodbye.

The warmth is contagious, a radiant jest,
The day looks around and feels quite the best.
With the sun's golden wink, the laughter ignites,
Creating a scene of pure silly sights.

Guiding Stars of the Wilderness

Under a blanket of twinkling dreams,
The owls wink at night, or so it seems.
Raccoons in masks raid a pantry so bright,
While fireflies flicker like stars caught in flight.

A moose trips over, a truly grand blunder,
And giggles erupt in the warm evening thunder.
The constellations chuckle, sharing old tales,
Of mischief and giggles across the moon trails.

Footprints in a Field of Gold

A chicken danced on fields so bright,
Clucking tunes that felt just right.
The cows joined in with mooing glee,
While pigs rolled in the grass carefree.

The gardener laughed, misplacing seeds,
Lost in thoughts of flower needs.
But flowers sprouted, wild and bold,
In chaos, beauty's dance unfolds.

Cascades of Happiness Unfurled

A brook babbles jokes with the breeze,
Tickling plants beneath the trees.
The frogs croak laughter, quite absurd,
As fish tell tales without a word.

Sunlight glitters like a prank,
On waters cool, they laugh and clank.
A picnic spreads, crumbs fly about,
With ants in suits, they dance about.

Parables of Peace in the Meadow

Grasshoppers share wisdom, quite witty,
While daisies gossip, oh so gritty.
A snail tells stories, though it's slow,
Of races lost with quite the show.

Butterflies wear colors so bright,
They flutter and tease with pure delight.
And squirrels plot mischief in the trees,
Chasing tails in the warm, soft breeze.

Celestial Connections

Stars wink down from their lofty heights,
While moonbeams giggle through the nights.
Comets race, but trip on air,
As constellations twist in flair.

Asteroids roll in a cosmic dance,
While planets gawk, caught in a trance.
Galaxies chuckle, spinning wide,
In a universe where dreams reside.

Wildflowers

Wildflowers bloom in chaos bright,
Dancing 'round, what a silly sight.
Their colors clash in a jester's show,
A carnival where breezes blow.

Bumblebees wear top hats and frown,
While petals twirl in a flower gown.
Each bloom with stories, bold and quirky,
Laughing softly, ever so jerky.

Cradle of Joy in Nature's Arms

The squirrels throw nuts like confetti,
While birds gossip on branches, so petty.
Frogs croak up songs, quite a few,
As turtles play tag in the morning dew.

The trees wear hats made of bright green leaves,
And flowers dance twirls in the warm breeze.
Bees buzz along, they're quite the chatter,
While butterflies flaunt, like fancy patter.

A rabbit hops by, he's dressed to impress,
With carrots in pocket, he's a true success.
Nature's humor, oh what a delight,
In this realm of giggles, everything's bright.

So come, my friend, let's laugh and play,
In this joyful world, day after day.
Where the sun winks down with a golden ray,
And happiness grows in the funniest way.

Sunkissed Wanderings of the Soul

A chipmunk plans his great escape,
With a treasure map drawn on a grape.
He stumbles, giggling at his own flair,
As the sunbeam tickles without a care.

The flowers gossip, they've got the scoop,
On a deer who thinks he's in a hoop.
He prances around, like he's won a crown,
Tripping on roots, then falling down.

Clouds drift by, with shapes that tease,
A pancake, a cat, and even some cheese.
They laugh at the travelers down below,
Who point and wonder, then shout "Whooa!"

The sun sets, but fun's not done,
With fireflies glowing, oh what a run!
Let's wander through night, in this dream parade,
Where every laugh adds to the charade.

A Tapestry of Dreams and Dawn

A rooster's crow hides a giggle or two,
While the sun stretches out in a sky so blue.
The daisies whisper their morning prayer,
While the sun frolics without a care.

A plucky little sheep sidesteps the grass,
Trying to dodge the hard-hitting sass.
He leaps like a dancer, all fluff and wool,
As the cows cheer him on—what a fool!

In a stream, reflections play peek-a-boo,
As frogs make a splash, in a jubilant brew.
The dragonflies giggle, their wings a blur,
Chasing dreams that make all hearts stir.

So gather around, with mirth in the air,
For a tapestry woven with laughter to share.
With each silly moment, let giggles drown,
In the hues of a dawn, our joyful crown.

Colors Blooming in Silent Reverie

In a garden where paintbrushes grow,
The daisies dip into colors that glow.
Sunflowers strut like they own the scene,
While violets giggle, dressed in between.

A gopher pops up with a grin on his face,
Waving to flowers in a bright, lively race.
He digs up a carrot big as his dream,
And shouts, "Look at my prize!" in a giddy beam.

The clouds overhead chuckle and tease,
Dropping sprinkles of water with playful ease.
The butterflies waltz in a dance so spry,
Making petals giggle, as time flies by.

So join in the fun, let your laughter sway,
In this colorful realm, where joy has its way.
Where each petal whispers secrets untold,
Colors blooming, in delight unfold.

The Gentle Caress of Waking Light

The rooster crows, the sun does peek,
The pillow hugs, I do not speak.
My dreams of donuts, jelly-filled,
Yet here I am, my coffee spilled.

The cat insists, it's time to play,
While I just wish to snooze all day.
With socks unmatched, I waddle 'round,
In morning's glow, we all are clowns.

The toast is burnt, the eggs are fried,
Heavenly breakfast—what a ride!
I tackle crumbs with napkin grace,
As laughter rolls upon my face.

Yet through the chaos, joy does bloom,
Like flowers growing in the gloom.
Amidst the giggles and the mess,
I find my heart in morning's dress.

Marigold Memories

At Grandma's house, with cookies sweet,
The marigolds dance, they're quite a treat.
With golden blooms in the warm sun's glow,
I sneak some snacks, but she does know.

Her apron thick with tales to tell,
Of dancing mice and laughter's spell.
She giggles loud as flour does fly,
And swats my hand when I sneak by.

With every bite, a memory spun,
Of reckless youth, and silly fun.
We'd chase the bees, and run so free,
Lost in a world made just for me.

So here I sit, with tea in hand,
In marigold fields, I make my stand.
Life's sweetest moments, so absurd,
In loving whispers, dreams are stirred.

The Oasis of Sighs

In a desert made of laundry piles,
I find my peace through clever smiles.
The socks revolt, the shirts unite,
While I attempt to fold them right.

The vacuum hums a tune so grand,
It's hard to dance, but I will stand.
With dust bunnies swirling in the air,
I'm quite the sight, just stop and stare.

A water break, I plan to sip,
But end up with the cup's wild trip.
Spilled lemonade, a sticky mess,
In my oasis, I must confess.

But laughter blooms beneath the grime,
As I embrace this wacky time.
In the heat of chores, there's a delight,
I revel in chaos, pure and bright.

Symphony of the Verdant

In a garden filled with silly blooms,
The veggies sing of their funny dooms.
The carrots dance, the peas do sway,
    While I just chuckle at their play.

The sunbeams tickle, the breeze does tease,
With butterflies waltzing through the trees.
I wander lost in this green ballet,
With mismatched shoes, oh what a day!

The tomatoes blush, they're quite a sight,
While daisies giggle in sheer delight.
I join their ranks, a merry tune,
In this soft chaos, I'm over the moon.

So here we are, a quirky crew,
In nature's laughter, skies so blue.
With every rustle, a joke does rise,
In this grand symphony, joy never dies.

Secrets of the Emerald Oasis

In a land where coconuts wear hats,
Monkeys trade secrets with gossiping chats.
The parakeets, they have a dance-off,
While the camels just pretend to scoff.

A cactus tried to sell me a rose,
Claimed it's a beauty that everyone knows.
The sand's too hot for barefooting pranks,
So we just laugh by the cool waterbanks.

A palm tree whispered, 'Check out my leaf!'
'It's quite a show, a true comic relief!'
We giggled as it wiggled with flair,
Even lizards thought it was quite rare.

So here, in this oasis so bright,
Every creature knows how to delight.
With laughter echoing through the air,
Who needs trouble when joy is so rare?

Sunlit Paths Through Celestial Fields

In fields where the daisies play peekaboo,
Grasshoppers wear tuxes – yes, it's true!
Sunny beams tickle every blade,
While bees hold dances to serenade.

Butterflies gossip, flitting about,
Saying, 'What's that bump? Oh, was it a doubt?'
The clouds are thinking of taking a nap,
While the daisies conspire to form a map.

Through sunlit paths, we may go astray,
Finding lost sandals that just want to play.
A squirrel with shades sips lemonade,
Declaring, 'I'll stay here, don't be afraid!'

So let's frolic where humor lies,
In the fields beneath the open skies.
With every step, a giggle will bloom,
And laughter ensures it's never a gloom.

The Melody of Forgotten Love

Once a heart sang tunes so bright,
But now it hums of humorous fright.
It reminisces in a silly way,
Of a past romance on a foggy day.

There's no need for roses or a fine dinner,
Just a joke or two for the true winner.
An old record skips, but it still plays tunes,
Of love's missteps under cartoon moons.

A couple laughed over burnt toast,
Claiming it's just an oven's boast.
With mismatched socks and silly shoes,
Their love's a comedy, never to lose.

So let the melody of laughter ring,
In the dance of silly, sweet everything.
For love might fade, but joy stays alive,
And in this funny tune, we all thrive.

Echoes from the Land of the Free

In a land where roosters are out of tune,
They crow at midnight, not just in June.
A raccoon claims he's the king of the trash,
While the squirrels make popcorn and have a bash.

Fireflies summon a glow-in-the-dark rave,
Where the night critters all dance and behave.
Jokes fly like arrows, with giggles galore,
And laughter's the language everyone should explore.

The grasshoppers hold court with their puns,
While the rabbits strategize for their runs.
A turtle reminds everyone to slow down,
And laughter spreads wide throughout the town.

So here we stand, with joy as our plea,
In echoes of laughter from land to sea.
With every chuckle, we find we are free,
In this whimsical world, just you and me.

Journeys through Sacred Landscapes

On trails where the squirrels mock,
I tripped over my own sock.
The cactus waved with a grin,
As a llama pranced right in.

Mountains chuckled, skies did tease,
Sipping rain from the blooming trees.
I wore a hat that was too bright,
And danced with shadows in delight.

Fields whispered tales, oh so grand,
While a goat asked for a hand.
I stumbled upon a river's song,
And laughed because nothing felt wrong.

With laughter echoing through the vale,
I forgot I was without a trail.
Each step became a playful jest,
In landscapes where joy feels blessed.

Metamorphosis of the Dawn

The sun popped up like a toast,
While chickens sang a morning boast.
It stretched its rays in silly ways,
While frogs leapt high in sunrise plays.

Dewdrops giggled on leaves so green,
As butterflies danced, slick and keen.
A snail took off with a sleepy cheer,
Chasing the light, then disappeared.

In the garden, the gnomes came alive,
Planning a race, they took a dive.
Waking dreams, in colors bright,
Turning morning into sheer delight.

As laughter dawned on sleepy heads,
And filled the air with silly spreads,
The world awakened with a smile,
In a whimsical, charming style.

Celestial Embrace

Stars fell down like party confetti,
While the moon danced, oh so petty.
It called the night for a playful spark,
Dragging clouds to join the lark.

Planets rolled in a playful game,
While comets insisted on a name.
Galaxies twirled in a silly fight,
Proving that chaos feels so right.

Asteroids chuckled, tumbling fast,
Eclipsing each other, shadows cast.
In this cosmos where laughter reigns,
Even the black holes have silly chains.

With each twinkle, a chuckle soared,
And dreams of space were well ignored.
In cosmic wonder, the silly beams,
Turned the night into dancing dreams.

Where Time Stands Still

In a land where clocks forgot to tick,
Penguins biked, doing tricks so slick.
Time sighed in a cozy chair,
While jellybeans floated in the air.

Each second became a joyful tease,
As turtles ran with the greatest ease.
Laughter echoed from each wall,
Joyful chaos, a siren's call.

Days and nights began to blend,
With giggles shared around each bend.
A clock struck twelve, then started to play,
As candy rain fell throughout the day.

In this realm of unhurried spree,
Come join the fun, just you and me.
With whimsy wrapped in laughter's thrill,
In moments caught where time stands still.

The Lullaby of Leaf and Stream

A leaf fell down, it took a ride,
On a stream that giggled, side to side.
It whispered jokes to the fish below,
Who wiggled and jiggled, putting on a show.

The brook chuckled loud, a bubbling cheer,
As squirrels danced, without a care,
They laughed at acorns, all in a row,
While birds made music, stealing the show.

The sun peeked in, a curious cat,
Who watched the splashes, where laughter sat.
The shadows tickled, as breezes swirled,
In this giggly world, where joy unfurled.

So if you wander near the stream,
Join the fun, it's quite a dream.
For here in nature, laughter gleams,
And life is nothing but silly themes.

Reveries in the Garden of Whimsy

In a garden where the daisies dance,
A gnome tripped over, lost his pants.
The butterflies giggled, fluttered in glee,
While frogs croaked jokes from a nearby tree.

The roses strutted in colors bold,
Telling tales of love, amusingly told.
While carrots in coats held a fancy soirée,
Pumpkins all laughed, come join the fray!

Sunbeams chuckled, tickling the air,
As clouds in cape capered without a care.
The rabbits played cards, so shifty and sly,
For in this garden, no one would cry.

So wander through laughter, let worries cease,
In this whimsical space, find your peace.
With joy blooming bright, jump in the scene,
In this laughter-filled land, be a queen!

The Horizon Where Hope Meets Dawn

A rooster crowed, oh what a sight,
As dawn tiptoed in, chasing the night.
The sun yawned wide, a golden grin,
While shadows danced, inviting a spin.

The horizon giggled, brushed with dreams,
While squirrels debated the best of creams.
They plotted and planned, a nutty affair,
A picnic of laughter, happiness to share.

The clouds wore hats, quite eccentric styles,
While daisies joined in, sporting their smiles.
With every ray that painted the sky,
Hope whispered softly, oh my, oh my!

So rise with the sun, let your joy expand,
Together we'll frolic, hand in hand.
For on this bright shore, together we play,
At the horizon's edge, we'll laugh all day.

An Odyssey Through Sunbeams and Serenity

Through sunbeams bright, a traveler grinned,
With socks mismatched, a daring win.
He danced past shadows, skipping along,
While birds chimed in with a silly song.

The trees waved hello, branches all tall,
As squirrels held court, reciting a call.
"Who's the king of this quirky land?"
They squeaked and squealed, a topsy turvy band.

A breeze hummed gently, coaxing a laugh,
As daisies leaned in, for a bit of a gaffe.
A sunbeam winked at this foolish spree,
While butterflies fluttered, giggling with glee.

So journey along through the gleeful way,
Where laughter and joy hold solid sway.
In this odyssey bright, let your spirit be free,
For the sunbeams and smiles wait for you and me.

Dancing with Shadows of Delight

In the grove where giggles play,
Shadows dance the day away,
With each step, they slip and slide,
Twisting fun with joyous pride.

Twilight brings a funny rhyme,
As we laugh, we lose all time,
The shadows tango, never shy,
With silly moves that catch the eye.

Underneath the moon's bright glare,
Laughter echoes everywhere,
Chasing shadows, play's the game,
In this dance, we're all the same.

So let's sway without a care,
In our playful, fragrant air,
Each shadow's laugh adds to the cheer,
Let's twirl around, my friend, come near!

When Flora Meets the Infinite Sky

Oh, the flowers have a chat,
'Is that a bee or just a hat?'
Petals giggle, colors boast,
As bees buzz in, they play host.

Up above, a cloud drifts by,
With a witty wink, oh my!
Butterflies in silly spins,
As nature laughs at all our sins.

Pollen parties, wild and free,
"Hey, come dance down here with me!"
But watch your step, don't trip on roots,
Or end up lost in flowered boots.

So when flora meets the sky,
Expect some giggles and a sigh,
For nature's antics will unroll,
And tickle that forgotten soul.

The Allure of Serendipitous Moments

Stumbling on a joyful tune,
Like finding socks, there's one, then two,
These moments come without a cue,
Sneaking smiles in the morning dew.

A butterfly with a flair to land,
Came by wearing a silly band,
It whispered secrets to my ear,
While squirrels laughed and gave a cheer.

Life unravels in whims and chance,
Every mishap leads to a dance,
So tip your hat to fate's embrace,
In this parade, we'll find our place.

With every surprise, we leap and sway,
In the garden where we play,
So let's toast to all that's grand,
And chase the laughter hand in hand!

Rapture Beneath the Starlit Tree

Underneath the tree so grand,
We gather round to form a band,
Chirping crickets keep the beat,
While shadows dance with wiggly feet.

Stars above are playful spies,
Winking down with twinkly eyes,
They chuckle softly, wrap the night,
As dreams take flight in pure delight.

With every branch, a story spins,
Of silly bugs and epic wins,
We gather tales from roots to crown,
With laughter echoing all around.

So let's enjoy this magic hour,
Awash in joy, sweet laughter's power,
Underneath the sprawling leaves,
For here, at night, our heart believes!

Dancing Shadows of Ferns

In the breeze, they twist and twirl,
Shadows of ferns, doing a whirl.
A squirrel joins in with a jig,
Eager to flaunt his little gig.

Grasshoppers hop, all in delight,
While caterpillars dance at night.
The sun peeks down, with a wink,
Inviting all to join and sync.

We laugh as the leaves begin to sway,
Even the flowers join the play.
In this fest of nature's cheer,
Who knew the woods could feel so dear?

A rabbit stumbles, into a spin,
Toppling over, but grinning wide with a grin.
With every shuffle, every dive,
These dancing shadows come alive!

Celestial Roots

Beneath the sky, the roots conspire,
Whispering secrets, fueled by fire.
Stars giggle down, from up so high,
At trees who dream of learning to fly.

Worms debate about their lunch,
While bugs practice for a big crunch.
The moon gives a nod with a grin,
Encouraging all to join in.

Clouds puff up, wearing a crown,
Teasing the flowers to dance around.
"Oh, look at us!" petals declare,
"Why should the roots have all the flair?"

A raccoon stumbles, blushing red,
Trying to join the ballet instead.
In this leafy, lively retort,
Nature chuckles in joyful sport!

Reflections on Water's Edge

Ripples giggle, tickling the shore,
As frogs leap high, making quite the score.
The fish wink up, with mischievous glee,
Planning pranks on the ants, you see.

A duck twirls 'round, thinking it's grand,
While a turtle watches, plotting his stand.
"Why dance on land when I can float?
Join me, friends, let's make a boat!"

The sun dips low, painting a scene,
While water bugs laugh at their own sheen.
"Life's like a dance, just follow the beat,
Especially if you want a snack to eat!"

A splash here, a splash there, full of cheer,
The puddles erupt with laughter, it's clear.
In this giggling water ballet,
Reflections show us that it's a playful day!

Petals and Promises

Petals flutter like little kites,
Chasing the wind through sunny sights.
Each bloom whispers a promise sweet,
"Join us in joy, it's a sunny treat!"

The bees buzz, trying to stay chic,
While butterflies flaunt their colors, unique.
"I'll show you mine, if you show me yours!"
They twirl and spin, all without chores.

Each flower giggles, swaying on stems,
Making new friends, oh, what gems!
"Let's plan a party, under the sun,
With laughter and joy, oh what fun!"

A breeze carries tales, both wild and bright,
Transforming petals into pure delight.
In this garden of humor and rhyme,
Promises bloom, ready for prime time!

The Sanctuary of Laughter and Light

Beneath the sun, where giggles ring,
The flowers bloom and butterflies sing.
A squirrel slips on fallen pear,
Cracks a nut without a care.

Laughter erupts from buzzing bees,
Tickled by the dancing leaves.
A frog on a lily, ready to leap,
Dreams of hops that make him weep.

In this space of playful cheer,
Even shadows wait to hear.
A jester's hat upon a tree,
Who knew branches loved to be free?

Stick figures on the ground do play,
Joining birds in the sunny day.
Beneath the bright and foolish sun,
We laugh, we play, all in good fun.

Whispers in the Breeze of Wonder

The wind whispers secrets, light as a feather,
Through trees that giggle, all in good weather.
A turtle on a rock, dressed in style,
Poses for selfies, with a cheeky smile.

The daisies wear spectacles, oh what a sight!
While ants do the tango, full of delight.
Clouds float by, sporting wacky hats,
Trading jokes with the knickknack cats.

A giraffe stretching, just to say hi,
Knocks over a birdhouse, oh my, oh my!
With each chuckle, nature sings,
As butterflies don their whimsical wings.

In the breeze of wonder, joy does abound,
With laughter and smiles all around.
Even a rock joins in with a grin,
A perfect place for mirth to begin.

Reflections on a Crystal Lake

By the lake, where the ripples spark,
Frogs play chess till the skies turn dark.
A fish jumps out, wearing a crown,
Declaring itself the king of the town!

The ducks waddle in a synchronized line,
Performing a dance that's simply divine.
While turtles float, with hats on their shells,
Sharing secrets only water dwells.

A mirror reflection of laughter so pure,
Draws giggles from rocks, that I'm pretty sure.
Even the sun dips low with a wink,
Casting shadows that dance and blink.

So come take a peek at this whimsical view,
Where nature's the comedian, charming and true.
Each splashing wave, a punchline of glee,
In the crystal lake, wild laughter runs free.

The Blissful Maze of Green Delights

In a maze made of emerald and cheer,
A rabbit plays hide-and-seek, oh dear!
With carrots as prizes, it's quite the affair,
While giggling gnomes pop up everywhere.

The hedgehogs roll, wearing hats on their backs,
Dodging the pranks of mischievous tracks.
A parade of mushrooms, in colorful shoes,
Whispering secrets to the sneaky blue jays.

A berry bush dressed up in polka dots,
Offers sweet treats to the silly snots.
Chasing butterflies with ribbons in hand,
The joy of this place is simply unplanned.

So wander through giggles and playful sights,
In the blissful maze of whimsical nights.
Where laughter is a path, and joy leads the way,
In this labyrinth of fun, we'll forever stay.

Tranquil Waters' Embrace

Beneath the palm trees, fish wear hats,
They gossip and giggle, like silly brats.
A turtle in shades lounges on a rock,
As ducks play poker, they love to mock.

The frogs host a party, all dressed in green,
They dance like they're stars in a movie scene.
Goldfish jump high, aiming for the moon,
While water lilies hum a jazzy tune.

The sun shakes its tail, making the waves laugh,
Crabs are the judges in this wacky half.
Every splash sparks joy, it's a comical sight,
In this funny kingdom, everything feels right.

So here by the water, let giggles uncoil,
Where laughter and sunshine meet for a while.
Join the parade of the quirkiest show,
In tranquil embrace, let your worries go.

Luminescence of Morning Glories

Morning glories wake up with a yawn,
Their petals stretch out like pajamas at dawn.
Bees buzz around, sporting tiny hats,
While butterflies giggle, landing like spats.

A squirrel in slippers steals seeds from the bowl,
He hides from the cat, who's lost all control.
The sun starts to tickle the flowers awake,
In this bright circus, where pranks are at stake.

The wind plays the flute, it's a jazzy affair,
With daisies in tutus dancing without care.
Each flower a dancer, twirls without a fee,
In a riot of colors, as wild as can be.

So let's cheer for the morn, with fun galore,
When the world seems silly, who could ask for more?
With morning glories bright, and laughs that ignite,
Every dawn is a party, a sheer delight.

Harmonies of Nature's Lullaby

The crickets chirp out their evening song,
While fireflies twinkle, all night long.
A raccoon in pajamas plays tambourine,
While owls in tuxedos keep time very keen.

Squirrels bring snacks, in their little knapsacks,
As frogs do a jig, and they never lack.
The trees sway gently, conducting the crew,
Creating a symphony, vibrant and true.

Every rustle and giggle, every hoot and puff,
Turns this woodland into a realm of fun stuff.
Where laughter is music, and joy is the beat,
Nature's lullaby makes life feel complete.

So gather your friends for this nightly delight,
Join critters and creatures as they dance in moonlight.
For in harmonies rich, both silly and free,
Every moment sings pure poetry.

Colorful Retreats of the Soul

In a patchwork meadow of colors so bright,
The daisies are giggling, what a funny sight!
The butterflies whisper, each secret a joke,
While a sleepy old bear dreams of honey and smoke.

A rainbow appears, wearing slippers of cheer,
The sky breaks into laughter, for all to hear.
Clouds join the fun, doing skip and a hop,
With sunshine as DJ, the music won't stop.

Each flower's a dancer, they sway by the breeze,
Tickling the grasses, they wiggle with ease.
The breeze tells a tale, full of giggles and grins,
In a world painted bright, where the fun never ends.

So come take a stroll through this colorful land,
Let laughter embrace you; it's simply quite grand.
For in retreats so vivid, let your spirit be whole,
And dance with the flowers, it's good for the soul.

The Garden of Forgotten Wishes

In a garden where shoes go to hide,
Forgotten wishes dance full of pride.
A frog in a hat sings with flair,
While daisies giggle, without a care.

The sun wears shades, it's quite a sight,
As tomatoes plot a garden fright.
They roll their eyes at the lonely spade,
And gossip about the weeds that invade.

The carrots hold a parade at noon,
With potatoes twirling to a silly tune.
A scarecrow snickers, arms spread wide,
As lambs giggle and sheep run outside.

So join the fun, don't be a grump,
In this wacky plot where veggies jump.
A sabbatical for the dreams we've buried,
In this garden where wishes are married.

When Stars Touch Earth

When stars touch down for a midnight spree,
They trip on grass, oh silly and free!
One twinkles bright, spills milk on the floor,
While another plays hopscotch by the door.

They laugh and tumble with moonlight glee,
Creating constellations like you wouldn't believe!
A comet steals cookies, not one but a bag,
As fireflies dance, the night's little brag.

The world below just can't comprehend,
How a shooting star became my best friend.
They share my popcorn and dance with me,
While planets applaud, oh what a sight to see!

So when you gaze up and wish with a sigh,
Remember those stars that slip from the sky.
They may just drop by for a snack or two,
Bringing laughter and joy, just for you.

Breath of the Seraphs

In the realm where laughter flies,
Seraphs breathe out all the sighs.
They tickle the clouds with playful cheer,
And play tag with the sun, oh dear!

With wings like feathers, they dart and weave,
Around jellybean trees, if you believe.
One seraph sneezed, it sprinkled gumdrops,
While giggles echoed, and nobody stops.

They glide past the moon at tea time fair,
Spilling lemonade in the cool night air.
Each sip a chuckle, each laugh a grin,
As they dab their wings and twirl, let's begin!

So come take part in this snicker spree,
Where the breath of the seraphs sets laughter free.
From fluffy clouds to the earth below,
Join the frolic and let your joy show!

Echoes from the Meadow

In a meadow where whispers bloom and sway,
Echoes giggle, come out to play.
A butterfly slips with a wink so sly,
As daisies chuckle, "Oh my, oh my!"

The grass has secrets, soft and spry,
A rabbit hops by with a pie in the sky.
He shouts to the clouds, "Want some of this?"
While the sun grins down with a playful kiss.

Crickets compose a lively tune,
To the rhythm of bees buzzing 'round like a boon.
The hills sway gently, with laughter to share,
As the wind tosses dreams in the evening air.

So dance through the echoes, let laughter lead,
In a meadow of joy, that's all that we need.
With each little chuckle that floats by the way,
Find the happiness that blooms in the day.

The Promised Haven

In a land where ice cream trees grow,
The rivers flow with soda, don't you know?
Clouds are made of marshmallows, fluffy and bright,
And golden suns shine, painting the night.

Squeaky toy crickets serenade the day,
While gummy bears dance in their playful sway.
The grass tickles toes, in hops we embark,
As we race with the snails, oh what a lark!

Bumblebees wear tiny hats, very dapper,
While butterflies giggle, a kaleidoscope flapper.
Every squirrel's a comedian, clever and spry,
Making the clouds burst with laughter up high.

So grab a cupcake and take a seat near the brook,
In this whimsical place, life's a fun storybook.
With no cares or worries, just laughter to chase,
Welcome to the haven, a sweet, silly space.

Secrets of Sunlit Valleys

Where bananas grow on trees made of gum,
And zebras wear stripes of glittering plum.
The breeze tickles flowers, they giggle and sway,
As squirrels tell tales of the funniest day.

Lollipop mountains peek over the hills,
While ants wear sunglasses, planning their thrills.
The sun winks knowingly, casting its rays,
On marshmallow lakes where the sweet dolphins play.

A secret cookbook of chocolate-chip dreams,
Where laughter flows like the trickling streams.
With dancing popcorn and karaoke bugs,
Every corner awaits with soft, silly hugs.

In this land of the bright and the sweet and absurd,
Every moment's captured, each giggle's heard.
So let's chase the rainbows and twirl in delight,
Here every day ends with a ticklish night.

A Tapestry of Abundance

In gardens where jellybeans grow on tall vines,
And sunshine tastes sweet like syrupy wines.
Jellyfish picnic on a blanket of cheese,
As ducks wear bow ties, doing as they please.

The pizza trees sway with pepperoni fresh,
While rabbits don capes, feeling quite posh.
A fountain of milkshake sparkles in the light,
As silly penguins engage in snowball fights.

The clouds play hopscotch with the stars up high,
In a realm where the orange moon winks from the sky.
With goblins who juggle and trolls who paint,
Life here is quirky, quaint, and yet faint.

So grab your ice cream and come take a seat,
On fragrant grass that tastes simply sweet.
In a swirl of colors, so vibrant, so grand,
We weave tales of laughter across this strange land.

Soft Radiance of Dusk

As the sun dips low, the sky twirls in hue,
With shades of cotton candy, a whimsical view.
Fireflies wear glow sticks, shining so bright,
As crickets play banjos into the night.

The trees whisper secrets to giggling streams,
While sleepy-eyed owls weave fantastical dreams.
A parade of night critters dance without care,
While skunks in tuxedos pass by in a flare.

Stars hang like ornaments, twinkling in glee,
While the moon hums softly, a sweet melody.
With marshmallow cushions, we lounge on the grass,
Trading jokes with the rabbits who merrily pass.

So let laughter echo through spaces so wide,
As we spin in the glow of the dusk's fun ride.
In this cheerful realm where the wild hearts play,
We'll dance with the fireflies 'til the break of day.

Whispers of Eden's Embrace

In a garden so bright, where flowers all talk,
A snail took a stroll, then tripped on a rock.
He cried, "Oh dear heavens! What a clumsy fate!"
While bees buzzed above, they just couldn't relate.

A monkey swung by, with a grin full of cheer,
And offered the snail a ride without fear.
"Hop on my back, we'll find some ripe bananas!"
But the snail just sighed, "I prefer my pajamas."

The flowers then whispered, with giggles that flowed,
"Why rush for bananas when you can just bloat?"
The snail blinked in shock, then laughed till he cried,
"In this quirky garden, there's nowhere to hide!"

So they danced with the breeze, in a wild, silly spree,
While the sun shone down, as bright as could be.
In a world full of laughter, and silly delight,
The snail found his groove—he was ready to kite!

Beneath the Canopy of Bliss

Under the trees, where the critters all play,
A squirrel lost his nut, and went quite astray.
He turned to a rabbit, with worry in eyes,
"Have you seen my snack? It was big, round, and flies!"

The rabbit just chuckled, with a twitch of his nose,
"Perhaps it was dinner, or maybe a hose!"
They searched high and low, 'neath the leaves ever green,

Finding nothing but laughter, and a potato! It seemed.

A turtle strolled by, snickering slow,
"You're searching for nuts? Why, just steal my glow!"
The squirrel, unimpressed, just rolled his own eye,
"Thanks for the thought, but I'd rather just fry!"

As the sun dipped low, with a wink and a grin,
They munched on the snacks that the skunks had brought in.
Under the canopy, where fun never quits,
They feasted on laughter, and enjoyed all the hits!

Serene Shores of Lost Dreams

At the edge of the sea, where the crabs dance so slick,
A fish told a tale, not knowing it was thick.
"I once swam so far, that I tickled a whale!"
The crabs looked bewildered, then burst into wail.

A seagull swooped down, with a snappy retort,
"Tickled a whale? My friend, what a sport!"
He fluffed up his feathers, and shared his own tale,
"I once lost my lunch, it was quite a big fail!"

The waves laughed it off, making ripples in glee,
As the sun set in orange, creating a spree.
"Why worry so much when the surf's on our side?"
Cried the fish with a wink, and they all opted to ride.

So they danced by the shore, in the cool evening air,
Creating new stories, and casting all cares.
In serene shores of whimsy, where the funny tides play,
They splashed and they laughed, living wild every day!

The Garden Where Time Stands Still

In a garden so grand, where the toads sing a tune,
A snail met a turtle, both dreaming 'til noon.
"What time is it now?" asked the slow-moving pair,
The sun just chuckled, "It's still, if you dare!"

The flowers all giggled, wearing crowns made of dew,
While the butterfly fluttered, all painted in hue.
"Time's just a prankster, it's really a tease!"
Said the wise old oak, swaying gently in the breeze.

The turtle then pondered, with a thoughtful bug stare,
"If time's merely jest, then we've nothing to bear!"
They danced with the daisies, in a whimsical trance,
And forgot all their worries, as they joined in the dance.

So the garden grew lively, with laughter and cheer,
As the creatures discovered there's nothing to fear.
In a place where the clock simply skipped on a thrill,
They laughed and they played, in the garden's sweet chill!

Secrets of the Twilit Glade

Beneath the leaves, where shadows play,
A squirrel tells jokes, come what may.
He giggles and hops with such delight,
While critters roll on in the fading light.

The frogs croak tunes that seem quite bold,
Singing of tales both silly and old.
One toads says, 'Life's a hop and a skip!'
What else can you do? Just take a trip!

The sun bows down, so soft and round,
With fireflies dancing, twirling around.
A rabbit wears glasses to read the stars,
And claims that they're really just fancy cars!

Among the trees, wild laughter grows,
They're spreading cheer, nobody knows.
So join the fun, leave worries behind,
In this wooded realm, joy's easy to find.

Elysian Whispers

Where flowers gossip in breezy tones,
A butterfly pranks, poking at bones.
With petals a-flutter, they brush and tease,
Making the dandelions sneeze with ease.

The sun spills honey on the grass below,
As ants march out, putting on a show.
'You should see our dance!' the ladybug brags,
While the beetles scoff, wearing snazzy rags.

A cloud's a pillow for dreams gone astray,
As the parakeets sport in a sunny array.
'Feathers are free, but the jokes? They're rare!'
As they wink and fluff their colorful hair.

In playful whispers, the breeze tells the tale,
Of giggling tunes that float on the gale.
With every chuckle, the world seems bright,
In this realm of laughter, all feels just right.

Embracing the Infinite

On the swings of fate, we sway and spin,
With laughter that bubbles from deep within.
A cat plays chess against the old crow,
While pondering life—'Does your nose really glow?'

The sun tickles clouds with golden beams,
As owls tell secrets in gentle streams.
A wise old turtle whispers a riddle,
'Why did the chicken cross? To find a middle!'

The breezes jest with the leaves on high,
'Can you tickle a cloud? Just give it a try!'
And while they laugh, strong branches sway,
Making room for joy, come out and play!

In the laughter's arms, the day becomes bright,
As shadows dance, taking flight.
Every giggle is magic, every smile shines,
In this place of whimsy, life intertwines.

Chronicles of a Hidden Cove

Down by the shore where the seashells chat,
A crab tells stories, oh what of that!
With tales of adventures of waves and tides,
He chuckles, 'Watch out! Here come the rides!'

The octopus plays cards with a wise old fish,
'With eight arms, my dear, I'm bound to win this!'
Each round a gamble, a splash of delight,
As dolphins dive in with leaps of height.

Sandcastles rise, and the gulls fly low,
Picking on fries that the beachgoers throw.
A sandpiper swoops, making everyone squeal,
'This is my stage! I'm the real deal!'

With laughter echoing, the tide rolls away,
As smiles and giggles fill up the bay.
Catch the wave of joy, let your spirit soar,
In this quirky cove, you've found the core.

Fables of Fertile Fields

In a field so green, not a care to be found,
A cow wore sunglasses, strutting around.
Chickens held meetings, all clucking in line,
Debating the best way to farm for some wine.

The pig got a smartphone, took selfies that shone,
While sheep braided wool for the latest iPhone.
They planted their crops with a shake of a hoof,
As rabbits rapped sweet tunes from a bed made of woof.

One day a fox, in a suit and a tie,
Gave speeches on morals, made all the cows cry.
But soon he was stumped by a hen in a hat,
Who asked, "Where's your lunch? Are you really a brat?"

So they all laughed and danced till the sun said goodnight,

In fields of pure joy, everything felt just right.
With fables that shone, on days bright and fine,
These critters found bliss, oh, sweet half-past nine.

Whispers of the Ancient Grove

In an ancient grove where the odd things do dwell,
A squirrel wore glasses and invented a shell.
Trees told old jokes in a rustling breeze,
While mushrooms were giggling, down on their knees.

A wise old owl, with a snort and a wink,
Said, "Life's like a riddle, or maybe a drink!"
The rabbits bartered carrots for puns, oh so slick,
While hedgehogs played chess, trying hard not to prick.

A dance-off arose, led by a dancing bee,
Spinning webs with spiders, such a sight to see!
The moon winked above with a flicker of light,
As critters danced wildly, celebrating the night.

In whispers they'd share all their most funny tales,
Where laughter and joy filled their leafy trails.
For in this old grove, where all spirits soar,
A world full of giggles forever encore!

Rapture Among Blossoms

Amidst blooms so bright, a bumblebee sighed,
"Why am I buzzing? I'm not even fried!"
Butterflies giggled at the bee's tiny plight,
As blossoms were busy, preparing for night.

The daisies played tag, while the roses rolled dice,
The lilies poured tea, just a tad over nice.
With pollen disguised as a magical dust,
They floated on whispers, in flowers they trust.

Along came a ladybug, wearing a crown,
Proclaiming her reign over petals and gown.
"Let's party!" she shouted, "with nectar and cheer!"
While bees broke the piñata, all buzzing in fear.

With laughter and joy swirling fragrant and sweet,
The blossoms held stories that none could defeat.
And rapture reigned loud, like a sweet little song,
In gardens adorned where the funny belongs!

The Sanctuary of Stillness

In the sanctuary where silence has flair,
A snail made a throne just to sit and to stare.
Turtles exchanged tales, moving oh so slow,
Plotting grand journeys to places they'd go.

"Why rush?" said the sloth, dangling on a vine,
"When life runs so slow, it's perfectly fine!"
A frog was a bard, singing soft serenades,
In a puddle of laughter that never quite fades.

Then came a loud parrot, squawking of plans,
To open a restaurant serving up cans.
The ducks quacked of recipes, far too bizarre,
While squirrels debated, what's best from a jar.

Yet stillness remained, like a comfy old chair,
Where nature took pauses, just breathing the air.
In this quirky haven, where humor won't cease,
The sanctuary thrived in a world full of peace.

Blossoms at Dusk

Petals dance as day turns to night,
Bugs start a band, wielding their light.
Laughter echoes, like echoes do,
As flowers giggle, sipping the dew.

A bee in a suit with a tie made of fluff,
Says, "This flower's just too much stuff!"
He buzzes around, lost in delight,
While the petals snicker, watching his flight.

Meadows of Dreams

Cows in pajamas, dreaming of cheese,
Dance on the grass, doing just as they please.
Sheep in a choir, singing out loud,
As the goats spin tales, impressing the crowd.

Bunnies with shades, sipping their tea,
While frogs in the pond keep time with a beat.
The sun starts to yawn, stretches its rays,
And the meadow giggles at all of their plays.

Echoing the Silence

A squirrel tells secrets to a nearby tree,
While shadows debate if they should flee.
The owls hoot wisdom, in their wise hats,
While the crickets chirp jokes about old rats.

Mice whisper softly, plotting their schemes,
As night wraps around them, soft as their dreams.
A breeze joins the chatter with whispers so sweet,
And silence just giggles at each little tweet.

Where the River Meets the Sky

Fish wear sunglasses on their watery spree,
While ducks crack jokes sipping tea, oh so free.
A turtle in shades, moves at a crawl,
He laughs at the seagull who trips in a fall.

The clouds float by in their marshmallow way,
As the sun tells stories of bright, shiny days.
And the river chuckles, reflecting the fun,
Where moments are silly, and laughter's a run.

www.ingramcontent.com/pod-product-compliance
Lightning Source LLC
Chambersburg PA
CBHW072129070526
44585CB00016B/1586